50 New Year's Recipes for Home

By: Kelly Johnson

Table of Contents

- Champagne Chicken
- Pomegranate Glazed Salmon
- Black-eyed Pea Soup
- Roasted Brussels Sprouts with Bacon
- Sparkling Cranberry Punch
- Honey Glazed Ham
- Baked Brie with Cranberry Sauce
- Shrimp Cocktail with Cocktail Sauce
- Prosciutto-Wrapped Asparagus
- Beef Tenderloin with Red Wine Sauce
- Citrus Salad with Champagne Vinaigrette
- Crab Stuffed Mushrooms
- Rosemary Roasted Potatoes
- Chocolate-Dipped Strawberries
- Champagne Jello Shots
- Stuffed Dates with Goat Cheese and Pistachios
- Smoked Salmon Canapés
- Mini Caprese Skewers
- Garlic Butter Shrimp
- Mushroom Risotto
- Blood Orange Margaritas
- Mini Quiche Lorraine
- Spinach and Artichoke Dip
- Lobster Bisque
- Mini Beef Wellingtons
- Blue Cheese and Walnut Crostini
- Cucumber Avocado Rolls
- Apple Cider Glazed Pork Tenderloin
- Shrimp Scampi Linguine
- Caprese Salad Skewers
- Raspberry Bellini
- Gruyere and Thyme Stuffed Mushrooms
- Antipasto Platter
- Pesto Pasta Salad
- Fig and Goat Cheese Crostini

- Coconut Shrimp with Mango Dipping Sauce
- Cranberry Brie Bites
- Spicy Tuna Tartare
- Glazed Meatballs
- Pear and Blue Cheese Salad
- Mini Crab Cakes
- Roasted Vegetable Platter
- Champagne Sorbet
- Stuffed Jalapeños with Cream Cheese and Bacon
- Beef Sliders with Caramelized Onions
- Pomegranate Mojitos
- Smoked Gouda and Apple Crostini
- Teriyaki Chicken Wings
- Chocolate Truffles
- Mini Fruit Tarts

Champagne Chicken

Ingredients:

- 4 boneless, skinless chicken breasts
- Salt and pepper, to taste
- 2 tablespoons olive oil
- 2 cloves garlic, minced
- 1 cup Champagne or sparkling wine
- 1/2 cup chicken broth
- 1/2 cup heavy cream
- 2 tablespoons Dijon mustard
- 2 tablespoons chopped fresh parsley, for garnish

Instructions:

Season the chicken breasts with salt and pepper on both sides.
In a large skillet, heat the olive oil over medium-high heat. Add the chicken breasts to the skillet and cook until golden brown on both sides, about 5-6 minutes per side. Remove the chicken from the skillet and set aside.
In the same skillet, add the minced garlic and cook for about 1 minute, until fragrant.
Pour the Champagne or sparkling wine into the skillet, scraping up any browned bits from the bottom of the pan with a wooden spoon.
Add the chicken broth to the skillet and bring the mixture to a simmer. Allow it to simmer for about 5 minutes, until slightly reduced.
Stir in the heavy cream and Dijon mustard, and return the chicken breasts to the skillet. Simmer for another 5-7 minutes, until the chicken is cooked through and the sauce has thickened.
Taste and adjust seasoning with salt and pepper if needed.
Garnish the chicken with chopped parsley before serving.
Serve the Champagne Chicken hot, with your choice of side dishes. Enjoy!

Pomegranate Glazed Salmon

Ingredients:

- 4 salmon fillets
- 1 cup pomegranate juice
- 1/4 cup honey
- 2 tablespoons soy sauce
- 2 cloves garlic, minced
- 1 teaspoon grated ginger
- Salt and pepper to taste
- Fresh pomegranate arils for garnish (optional)
- Chopped parsley or green onions for garnish (optional)

Instructions:

Preheat oven: Preheat your oven to 375°F (190°C).
Prepare glaze: In a small saucepan, combine the pomegranate juice, honey, soy sauce, minced garlic, and grated ginger. Bring the mixture to a simmer over medium heat. Allow it to simmer gently until it reduces and thickens slightly, about 10-15 minutes. Season with salt and pepper to taste.
Prepare salmon: Season the salmon fillets with salt and pepper on both sides. Place the salmon fillets on a baking sheet lined with parchment paper or foil, skin side down.
Glaze the salmon: Brush the pomegranate glaze generously over the salmon fillets, coating them evenly.
Bake: Transfer the baking sheet to the preheated oven and bake the salmon for about 12-15 minutes, or until the salmon is cooked through and flakes easily with a fork. The exact cooking time may vary depending on the thickness of your salmon fillets.
Serve: Once the salmon is cooked, remove it from the oven and let it rest for a few minutes. Serve the glazed salmon hot, garnished with fresh pomegranate arils, chopped parsley, or green onions if desired.

Enjoy your delicious pomegranate glazed salmon as a flavorful and nutritious main dish!

Black-eyed Pea Soup

Ingredients:

- 1 tablespoon olive oil
- 1 onion, diced
- 2 cloves garlic, minced
- 2 carrots, diced
- 2 celery stalks, diced
- 1 bell pepper, diced (any color)
- 1 cup dried black-eyed peas, soaked overnight and drained
- 4 cups vegetable or chicken broth
- 1 can (14 oz) diced tomatoes
- 1 teaspoon dried thyme
- 1 teaspoon dried oregano
- 1/2 teaspoon smoked paprika
- Salt and pepper to taste
- Chopped fresh parsley for garnish (optional)

Instructions:

Prepare the black-eyed peas: Rinse the dried black-eyed peas and soak them in water overnight. Drain them before using.

Sauté aromatics: Heat the olive oil in a large pot over medium heat. Add the diced onion and cook until softened, about 5 minutes. Add the minced garlic and cook for another minute until fragrant.

Add vegetables: Add the diced carrots, celery, and bell pepper to the pot. Cook, stirring occasionally, until the vegetables begin to soften, about 5-7 minutes.

Add black-eyed peas and broth: Add the soaked and drained black-eyed peas to the pot, along with the vegetable or chicken broth. Bring the mixture to a boil, then reduce the heat to low and let it simmer, partially covered, for about 45 minutes to 1 hour, or until the black-eyed peas are tender.

Add tomatoes and spices: Stir in the diced tomatoes (with their juices), dried thyme, dried oregano, smoked paprika, salt, and pepper. Simmer the soup for an additional 15-20 minutes to allow the flavors to meld together.

Adjust seasoning and serve: Taste the soup and adjust the seasoning with salt and pepper if needed. Ladle the black-eyed pea soup into bowls, garnish with chopped fresh parsley if desired, and serve hot.

This black-eyed pea soup is delicious on its own or served with crusty bread for a complete meal. Enjoy!

Roasted Brussels Sprouts with Bacon

Ingredients:

- 1 lb Brussels sprouts, trimmed and halved
- 4-6 slices bacon, diced
- 2 tablespoons olive oil
- Salt and pepper to taste
- Optional: Balsamic glaze or grated Parmesan cheese for garnish

Instructions:

Preheat the oven: Preheat your oven to 400°F (200°C).

Prepare the Brussels sprouts: Trim the ends off the Brussels sprouts and cut them in half lengthwise. Remove any loose or discolored outer leaves. Place the halved Brussels sprouts in a large mixing bowl.

Cook the bacon: In a skillet over medium heat, cook the diced bacon until it becomes crispy and golden brown. Use a slotted spoon to transfer the cooked bacon to a plate lined with paper towels to drain excess grease. Reserve about 1 tablespoon of bacon fat in the skillet.

Toss with olive oil: Drizzle the olive oil over the Brussels sprouts in the mixing bowl. Season with salt and pepper to taste. Toss the Brussels sprouts until they are evenly coated with the oil and seasoning.

Roast in the oven: Spread the Brussels sprouts in a single layer on a baking sheet lined with parchment paper or aluminum foil. Make sure they are cut-side down for better caramelization. Place the baking sheet in the preheated oven and roast the Brussels sprouts for about 20-25 minutes, or until they are tender and golden brown, stirring once halfway through cooking.

Combine with bacon: Once the Brussels sprouts are roasted to your desired level of doneness, remove them from the oven and transfer them to a serving dish. Add the crispy bacon to the roasted Brussels sprouts and toss gently to combine.

Serve: Transfer the roasted Brussels sprouts with bacon to a serving platter. If desired, drizzle with balsamic glaze or sprinkle with grated Parmesan cheese before serving.

Enjoy your delicious roasted Brussels sprouts with bacon as a side dish to complement any meal!

Sparkling Cranberry Punch

Ingredients:

- 4 cups cranberry juice
- 2 cups orange juice
- 1 cup pineapple juice
- 1/4 cup fresh lemon juice
- 1/4 cup fresh lime juice
- 2 cups ginger ale or lemon-lime soda, chilled
- Fresh cranberries and citrus slices for garnish (optional)
- Ice cubes

Instructions:

Mix the juices: In a large punch bowl or pitcher, combine the cranberry juice, orange juice, pineapple juice, fresh lemon juice, and fresh lime juice. Stir well to combine.
Chill: If your juices are not already chilled, you can refrigerate the mixture for at least an hour to ensure it's cold.
Add the sparkling beverage: Just before serving, pour the chilled ginger ale or lemon-lime soda into the punch mixture. Stir gently to combine.
Garnish: Add ice cubes to the punch bowl or glasses. Optionally, garnish the punch with fresh cranberries and slices of citrus fruits like oranges, lemons, or limes for a festive touch.
Serve: Ladle the sparkling cranberry punch into glasses and serve immediately.

Enjoy your sparkling cranberry punch as a delightful and refreshing beverage for any occasion! If you're serving a crowd, you can easily double or triple the recipe to accommodate more guests.

Honey Glazed Ham

Ingredients:

- 1 bone-in ham (7-9 pounds)
- 1 cup honey
- 1/2 cup brown sugar
- 1/4 cup Dijon mustard
- 2 tablespoons apple cider vinegar
- 1 teaspoon ground cloves
- 1 teaspoon ground cinnamon
- Whole cloves (optional, for garnish)
- Pineapple rings and maraschino cherries (optional, for garnish)

Instructions:

Preheat the oven: Preheat your oven to 325°F (160°C).
Prepare the ham: Place the ham in a roasting pan, flat side down. Score the surface of the ham in a diamond pattern with a sharp knife, making cuts about 1/4 inch deep. If desired, insert whole cloves into the center of each diamond.
Make the glaze: In a small saucepan, combine the honey, brown sugar, Dijon mustard, apple cider vinegar, ground cloves, and ground cinnamon. Cook over medium heat, stirring constantly, until the mixture is smooth and the sugar has dissolved. Remove from heat.
Glaze the ham: Brush the honey glaze generously over the surface of the ham, making sure to coat it evenly.
Bake the ham: Place the glazed ham in the preheated oven and bake for about 15-18 minutes per pound, or until the internal temperature reaches 140°F (60°C) when measured with a meat thermometer inserted into the thickest part of the ham, avoiding contact with the bone.
Baste the ham: Every 30 minutes or so, baste the ham with the pan juices and glaze to keep it moist and flavorful.
Add garnishes (optional): About 30 minutes before the ham is done, you can add pineapple rings and maraschino cherries to the surface of the ham, securing them with toothpicks if necessary.
Rest and serve: Once the ham reaches the desired temperature, remove it from the oven and let it rest for about 10-15 minutes before slicing. This allows the juices to redistribute.

Slice and serve: Carve the ham into slices and serve warm. You can serve any remaining glaze on the side as a sauce.

Enjoy your delicious honey glazed ham as the centerpiece of your meal!

Baked Brie with Cranberry Sauce

Ingredients:

- 1 wheel of brie cheese (about 8-12 ounces)
- 1/2 cup cranberry sauce (homemade or store-bought)
- 1/4 cup chopped pecans or walnuts (optional)
- 1 tablespoon honey (optional)
- Crackers, sliced baguette, or apple slices for serving

Instructions:

Preheat the oven: Preheat your oven to 350°F (175°C).
Prepare the brie: Place the wheel of brie on a parchment paper-lined baking sheet or in a small oven-safe dish.
Score the top: Using a sharp knife, lightly score the top rind of the brie in a crosshatch pattern. This will help the cheese melt more evenly.
Add cranberry sauce: Spoon the cranberry sauce over the top of the brie, spreading it evenly to cover the surface. If desired, you can also drizzle a tablespoon of honey over the cranberry sauce for added sweetness.
Optional toppings: Sprinkle the chopped pecans or walnuts over the cranberry sauce for added texture and flavor.
Bake the brie: Place the prepared brie in the preheated oven and bake for 10-12 minutes, or until the cheese is soft and gooey, and the cranberry sauce is bubbly.
Serve: Once baked, carefully transfer the baked brie to a serving platter. Serve it immediately with crackers, sliced baguette, or apple slices for dipping.
Enjoy: Invite your guests to dig in and enjoy the creamy, melted brie paired with the sweet and tangy cranberry sauce.

Baked brie with cranberry sauce is a perfect appetizer for holiday gatherings, parties, or any special occasion. It's sure to be a hit with your guests!

Shrimp Cocktail with Cocktail Sauce

Ingredients:

For the shrimp:

- 1 lb large shrimp, peeled and deveined, tails left on
- 1 lemon, sliced
- 2 bay leaves
- Ice

For the cocktail sauce:

- 1/2 cup ketchup
- 2 tablespoons prepared horseradish
- 1 tablespoon lemon juice
- 1 teaspoon Worcestershire sauce
- Tabasco sauce, to taste (optional)
- Salt and freshly ground black pepper, to taste

For garnish (optional):

- Fresh parsley, chopped
- Lemon wedges

Instructions:

Prepare the shrimp: Fill a large pot with water and add lemon slices and bay leaves. Bring the water to a boil over high heat. Once boiling, add the shrimp and cook for 2-3 minutes, or until they turn pink and opaque. Be careful not to overcook them.

Shock the shrimp: Drain the shrimp and immediately transfer them to a bowl of ice water to stop the cooking process. Once cooled, drain the shrimp and pat them dry with paper towels. Transfer the shrimp to a plate or platter and refrigerate until ready to serve.

Make the cocktail sauce: In a small bowl, combine the ketchup, prepared horseradish, lemon juice, Worcestershire sauce, and Tabasco sauce (if using).

Stir well to combine. Season with salt and pepper to taste. Adjust the ingredients according to your taste preferences, adding more horseradish or Tabasco for extra heat if desired.

Chill the cocktail sauce: Cover the bowl of cocktail sauce with plastic wrap and refrigerate it for at least 30 minutes to allow the flavors to meld together.

Serve: Arrange the chilled shrimp on a serving platter or individual cocktail glasses. Place a small bowl of cocktail sauce in the center or distribute it among smaller serving dishes.

Garnish (optional): Garnish the shrimp cocktail with chopped fresh parsley and lemon wedges for an extra touch of freshness and flavor.

Enjoy: Serve the shrimp cocktail with the chilled cocktail sauce and enjoy this classic appetizer with friends and family!

Shrimp cocktail with cocktail sauce is a timeless appetizer that's sure to impress your guests at any gathering or party.

Prosciutto-Wrapped Asparagus

Ingredients:

- 1 lb (450g) asparagus spears, tough ends trimmed
- 6-8 slices prosciutto, thinly sliced
- Olive oil, for drizzling
- Freshly ground black pepper, to taste
- Balsamic glaze (optional), for drizzling
- Toothpicks (optional)

Instructions:

Preheat the oven: Preheat your oven to 400°F (200°C).
Prepare the asparagus: Wash the asparagus spears and trim off the tough ends. If the spears are thick, you may want to peel the bottom halves to ensure tenderness.
Wrap with prosciutto: Take one slice of prosciutto and cut it lengthwise into two strips. Wrap each strip of prosciutto tightly around an asparagus spear, starting from the bottom and working your way up to the tip. Repeat with the remaining asparagus spears and prosciutto slices.
Arrange on a baking sheet: Place the prosciutto-wrapped asparagus spears on a baking sheet lined with parchment paper or aluminum foil. Make sure to leave a little space between each spear.
Drizzle with olive oil: Drizzle the prosciutto-wrapped asparagus with olive oil, ensuring that each spear is lightly coated. Season with freshly ground black pepper to taste.
Bake: Transfer the baking sheet to the preheated oven and bake the prosciutto-wrapped asparagus for about 10-12 minutes, or until the asparagus is tender and the prosciutto is crispy.
Optional: If desired, you can broil the asparagus for an additional 1-2 minutes at the end to crisp up the prosciutto even more.
Serve: Once cooked, remove the prosciutto-wrapped asparagus from the oven and transfer them to a serving platter. If desired, drizzle with balsamic glaze for extra flavor.
Optional: If you used toothpicks to secure the prosciutto, remember to remove them before serving.
Enjoy: Serve the prosciutto-wrapped asparagus as a delicious appetizer or side dish, and enjoy the wonderful combination of flavors and textures!

Prosciutto-wrapped asparagus is not only delicious, but it's also quick and easy to prepare, making it perfect for entertaining or enjoying as a special treat any day of the week.

Beef Tenderloin with Red Wine Sauce

Ingredients:

For the beef tenderloin:

- 2 lbs (900g) beef tenderloin, trimmed and tied
- 2 tablespoons olive oil
- Salt and freshly ground black pepper, to taste

For the red wine sauce:

- 1 tablespoon olive oil
- 1 shallot, finely chopped
- 2 cloves garlic, minced
- 1 cup red wine (such as Cabernet Sauvignon or Merlot)
- 1 cup beef broth
- 2 tablespoons unsalted butter
- 1 tablespoon all-purpose flour (optional, for thickening)
- Salt and freshly ground black pepper, to taste

Instructions:

Preheat the oven: Preheat your oven to 425°F (220°C).

Prepare the beef tenderloin: Pat the beef tenderloin dry with paper towels. Rub the tenderloin all over with olive oil, then season generously with salt and freshly ground black pepper.

Sear the beef: Heat a large oven-safe skillet over medium-high heat. Once hot, add the beef tenderloin to the skillet and sear it on all sides until nicely browned, about 2-3 minutes per side.

Roast the beef: Transfer the skillet with the seared beef tenderloin to the preheated oven. Roast the beef for about 15-20 minutes, or until it reaches your desired level of doneness. For medium-rare, aim for an internal temperature of 130-135°F (55-57°C) when measured with a meat thermometer inserted into the thickest part of the tenderloin.

Rest the beef: Once cooked to your liking, remove the beef tenderloin from the oven and transfer it to a cutting board. Tent it loosely with aluminum foil and let it rest for about 10 minutes before slicing. This allows the juices to redistribute, resulting in a juicier and more flavorful steak.

Make the red wine sauce: While the beef is resting, prepare the red wine sauce. In the same skillet used to sear the beef, heat a tablespoon of olive oil over medium heat. Add the chopped shallot and minced garlic, and sauté until softened and fragrant, about 2-3 minutes.

Deglaze the skillet: Pour in the red wine, scraping up any browned bits from the bottom of the skillet with a wooden spoon or spatula. Allow the wine to simmer and reduce by half, about 5-7 minutes.

Add the beef broth: Stir in the beef broth and continue to simmer the sauce until it thickens slightly, about 5 minutes.

Thicken the sauce (optional): If desired, you can thicken the sauce further by whisking together 2 tablespoons of unsalted butter with 1 tablespoon of all-purpose flour until smooth. Add this mixture to the simmering sauce and whisk continuously until thickened.

Season and serve: Season the red wine sauce with salt and freshly ground black pepper to taste. Slice the rested beef tenderloin into thick slices and arrange them on a serving platter. Spoon the red wine sauce over the sliced beef, or serve it on the side as a dipping sauce.

Garnish and enjoy: Garnish the beef tenderloin with fresh herbs like chopped parsley or thyme, if desired. Serve immediately and enjoy your elegant and delicious beef tenderloin with red wine sauce!

This beef tenderloin with red wine sauce is sure to impress your guests and make any meal feel like a special occasion. Enjoy!

Citrus Salad with Champagne Vinaigrette

Ingredients:

For the salad:

- 4 cups mixed salad greens (such as baby spinach, arugula, or mixed greens)
- 2 oranges (any variety), peeled and segmented
- 2 grapefruits (any variety), peeled and segmented
- 1 small red onion, thinly sliced
- 1/4 cup sliced almonds, toasted
- 1/4 cup crumbled feta cheese (optional)
- Fresh mint leaves, for garnish (optional)

For the champagne vinaigrette:

- 1/4 cup champagne vinegar
- 1 tablespoon Dijon mustard
- 1 tablespoon honey
- 1/2 cup extra virgin olive oil
- Salt and freshly ground black pepper, to taste

Instructions:

Prepare the salad greens: In a large salad bowl, combine the mixed salad greens of your choice. You can use baby spinach, arugula, mixed greens, or a combination of your favorite leafy greens.

Prepare the citrus fruits: Using a sharp knife, carefully peel the oranges and grapefruits, removing all the white pith. Slice the fruits into segments, removing any seeds or membranes.

Assemble the salad: Arrange the citrus segments on top of the mixed greens in the salad bowl. Add the thinly sliced red onion on top. Sprinkle the toasted sliced almonds over the salad. If using, scatter the crumbled feta cheese on top for added flavor.

Make the champagne vinaigrette: In a small bowl or jar, whisk together the champagne vinegar, Dijon mustard, and honey until well combined. Slowly drizzle in the extra virgin olive oil while whisking continuously to emulsify the dressing. Season with salt and freshly ground black pepper to taste.

Dress the salad: Drizzle the champagne vinaigrette over the citrus salad, tossing gently to coat the greens and fruits evenly with the dressing. Be careful not to overdress the salad; you can always add more dressing later if needed.

Garnish and serve: Garnish the citrus salad with fresh mint leaves for a pop of color and extra freshness, if desired. Serve immediately as a light and refreshing appetizer or side dish.

Enjoy: Enjoy your citrus salad with champagne vinaigrette as a delicious and vibrant addition to any meal. It's perfect for brunch, lunch, or as a starter for a special dinner!

This citrus salad is not only beautiful and flavorful but also packed with vitamins and antioxidants, making it a healthy and refreshing choice for any occasion.

Crab Stuffed Mushrooms

Ingredients:

- 12 large mushrooms, cleaned with stems removed
- 8 oz (225g) lump crabmeat, drained and picked over for shells
- 4 oz (115g) cream cheese, softened
- 1/4 cup grated Parmesan cheese
- 2 cloves garlic, minced
- 2 green onions, thinly sliced
- 1 tablespoon fresh lemon juice
- 1/2 teaspoon Worcestershire sauce
- 1/4 teaspoon Old Bay seasoning (optional)
- Salt and freshly ground black pepper, to taste
- 2 tablespoons chopped fresh parsley, for garnish
- Lemon wedges, for serving (optional)

Instructions:

Preheat the oven: Preheat your oven to 375°F (190°C).

Prepare the mushrooms: Remove the stems from the mushrooms and discard or reserve for another use. Use a spoon to gently scrape out the gills from the mushroom caps to create more room for the filling. Place the mushroom caps on a baking sheet lined with parchment paper or aluminum foil.

Prepare the filling: In a mixing bowl, combine the lump crabmeat, softened cream cheese, grated Parmesan cheese, minced garlic, sliced green onions, fresh lemon juice, Worcestershire sauce, and Old Bay seasoning (if using). Season with salt and freshly ground black pepper to taste. Mix well to combine all the ingredients evenly.

Stuff the mushrooms: Spoon the crab mixture into the mushroom caps, dividing it evenly among them and mounding it slightly.

Bake the stuffed mushrooms: Transfer the baking sheet with the stuffed mushrooms to the preheated oven and bake for about 15-20 minutes, or until the filling is heated through and the mushrooms are tender.

Garnish and serve: Once baked, remove the stuffed mushrooms from the oven and transfer them to a serving platter. Sprinkle the chopped fresh parsley over the top for garnish. Serve the stuffed mushrooms hot, with lemon wedges on the side for squeezing over the top if desired.

Enjoy: Serve the crab stuffed mushrooms as a delicious appetizer for your guests to enjoy. They're sure to be a hit at any party or gathering!

These crab stuffed mushrooms are bursting with flavor and make an elegant appetizer that's sure to impress. Enjoy!

Rosemary Roasted Potatoes

Ingredients:

- 2 pounds (about 900g) potatoes (such as Yukon Gold or red potatoes), washed and cut into bite-sized pieces
- 2 tablespoons olive oil
- 2 cloves garlic, minced
- 1 tablespoon fresh rosemary leaves, chopped (or 1 teaspoon dried rosemary)
- Salt and freshly ground black pepper, to taste
- Optional: Parmesan cheese, grated, for serving

Instructions:

Preheat the oven: Preheat your oven to 425°F (220°C).
Prepare the potatoes: Wash the potatoes thoroughly and cut them into bite-sized pieces. You can peel them if desired, but leaving the skins on adds texture and flavor. Pat the potato pieces dry with a paper towel to remove excess moisture.
Season the potatoes: In a large bowl, toss the potato pieces with olive oil, minced garlic, chopped rosemary leaves, salt, and freshly ground black pepper until evenly coated.
Roast the potatoes: Spread the seasoned potatoes in a single layer on a baking sheet lined with parchment paper or aluminum foil, ensuring that they are not overcrowded. This allows them to roast evenly and become crispy.
Bake in the oven: Place the baking sheet in the preheated oven and roast the potatoes for about 30-35 minutes, or until they are golden brown and crispy on the outside, and tender on the inside. Be sure to stir the potatoes halfway through the cooking time to ensure even browning.
Serve: Once the potatoes are done, remove them from the oven and transfer them to a serving dish. Optionally, sprinkle grated Parmesan cheese over the roasted potatoes before serving for an extra burst of flavor.
Enjoy: Serve the rosemary roasted potatoes hot as a delicious side dish alongside your favorite main course. They're perfect for pairing with grilled or roasted meats, poultry, or even as part of a vegetarian meal.

These rosemary roasted potatoes are simple to make and full of flavor, making them a versatile and satisfying addition to any meal.

Chocolate-Dipped Strawberries

Ingredients:

- Fresh strawberries, washed and dried
- Dark, milk, or white chocolate (whichever you prefer)
- Optional: chopped nuts, sprinkles, shredded coconut, or any other toppings you like

Instructions:

Prepare the Strawberries: Make sure your strawberries are thoroughly washed and dried. It's essential to dry them completely to ensure the chocolate sticks well.

Melt the Chocolate: Chop the chocolate into small, uniform pieces for easy melting. You can do this using a microwave or a double boiler on the stove. If using a microwave, heat the chocolate in short intervals, stirring in between until smooth and melted. If using a double boiler, place the chocolate in the top bowl over simmering water, stirring constantly until melted.

Dip the Strawberries: Holding each strawberry by the stem, dip it into the melted chocolate, swirling to coat it completely. Allow any excess chocolate to drip off back into the bowl.

Add Toppings (Optional): While the chocolate is still wet, you can roll the dipped strawberries in chopped nuts, sprinkles, shredded coconut, or any other toppings you like. Place the decorated strawberries on a parchment-lined baking sheet or plate.

Chill: Once all the strawberries are dipped and decorated, place them in the refrigerator to chill for at least 30 minutes or until the chocolate sets completely.

Serve: Once the chocolate has set, your chocolate-dipped strawberries are ready to be enjoyed! Serve them as a delicious dessert or snack.

These chocolate-dipped strawberries are perfect for special occasions like Valentine's Day, anniversaries, or any time you're craving a sweet treat. Enjoy!

Champagne Jello Shots

Ingredients:

- 1 cup champagne or sparkling wine
- 1 cup boiling water
- 2 envelopes (14g) unflavored gelatin
- 1/4 cup sugar (adjust to taste)
- Fresh fruit (optional, for garnish)

Instructions:

Prepare Gelatin Mixture: In a mixing bowl, pour the boiling water over the unflavored gelatin powder. Stir until the gelatin is completely dissolved.
Add Sugar: Stir in the sugar until it's fully dissolved. Adjust the amount of sugar to your taste preference. If you prefer sweeter shots, you can add more sugar.
Mix in Champagne: Pour the champagne into the gelatin mixture. Stir well to combine.
Pour into Shot Glasses: Carefully pour the mixture into shot glasses or silicone molds. Fill them about 3/4 of the way full.
Chill: Place the shot glasses or molds in the refrigerator to set. This usually takes about 2-4 hours, but it's best to check them periodically.
Garnish (optional): Once the Jello shots are set, you can garnish them with fresh fruit, such as berries or citrus slices, for an extra touch of elegance.
Serve: Once fully set, your Champagne Jello shots are ready to be enjoyed! Serve them chilled and have fun.

These Champagne Jello shots are perfect for parties, celebrations, or any occasion where you want to add a bit of sparkle to your festivities. Enjoy responsibly!

Stuffed Dates with Goat Cheese and Pistachios

Ingredients:

- Medjool dates (as many as you'd like to prepare)
- Goat cheese
- Pistachios (shelled and chopped)
- Honey (optional, for drizzling)

Instructions:

Prepare the Dates: Using a small knife, make a lengthwise slit along one side of each date. Carefully remove the pit from each date.
Stuff with Goat Cheese: Take a small amount of goat cheese and stuff it into the cavity of each date. You can use a spoon or your fingers to do this.
Add Pistachios: Sprinkle chopped pistachios on top of the goat cheese in each date. Press gently to make sure they adhere to the cheese.
Optional Drizzle: If desired, drizzle a small amount of honey over the stuffed dates. This adds a touch of sweetness to complement the savory goat cheese and nuttiness of the pistachios.
Serve: Arrange the stuffed dates on a serving platter and serve immediately. They can be enjoyed as a snack, appetizer, or even as part of a cheese board.

These stuffed dates are a delicious and elegant addition to any gathering or party. They offer a perfect balance of flavors and textures that are sure to impress your guests. Enjoy!

Smoked Salmon Canapés

Ingredients:

- Thinly sliced smoked salmon
- Baguette or crackers
- Cream cheese or goat cheese
- Fresh dill (optional, for garnish)
- Lemon wedges (optional, for serving)

Instructions:

Prepare the Base: If using a baguette, slice it into thin rounds. Alternatively, you can use crackers as the base for your canapés.

Spread Cheese: Take each baguette round or cracker and spread a thin layer of cream cheese or goat cheese on top. The creaminess of the cheese will provide a nice contrast to the salty smoked salmon.

Add Smoked Salmon: Place a piece of thinly sliced smoked salmon on top of each cheese-covered base. You can fold or arrange the salmon in a decorative manner if desired.

Garnish: If using, garnish each canapé with a small sprig of fresh dill. Dill complements the flavors of smoked salmon beautifully and adds a pop of color.

Serve: Arrange the smoked salmon canapés on a serving platter and serve immediately. Optionally, you can serve them with lemon wedges on the side for squeezing over the canapés just before eating.

These smoked salmon canapés are perfect for parties, brunches, or any gathering where you want to impress your guests with a sophisticated yet easy-to-make appetizer. Enjoy!

Mini Caprese Skewers

Ingredients:

- Cherry tomatoes
- Fresh mozzarella balls (bocconcini)
- Fresh basil leaves
- Balsamic glaze (optional, for drizzling)
- Toothpicks or small skewers

Instructions:

Prepare Ingredients: Wash the cherry tomatoes and basil leaves. Drain the mozzarella balls if they were stored in liquid.

Assemble Skewers: Take a toothpick or small skewer and thread on one cherry tomato, followed by a mozzarella ball, and finally a fresh basil leaf. Repeat this process until you've used up all your ingredients.

Arrange on Platter: Place the assembled mini Caprese skewers on a serving platter. You can arrange them in a neat row or create a decorative pattern.

Optional Drizzle: If desired, drizzle balsamic glaze over the skewers just before serving. The balsamic glaze adds a touch of sweetness and tanginess that complements the flavors of the tomatoes, mozzarella, and basil.

Serve: Mini Caprese skewers can be served immediately at room temperature. They make for a beautiful and tasty appetizer that's sure to impress your guests.

These mini Caprese skewers are not only visually appealing but also bursting with flavor. They're a perfect bite-sized treat for any occasion. Enjoy!

Garlic Butter Shrimp

Ingredients:

- 1 pound large shrimp, peeled and deveined
- 4 tablespoons unsalted butter
- 4 cloves garlic, minced
- 1 tablespoon olive oil
- Salt and pepper to taste
- 2 tablespoons chopped fresh parsley
- Lemon wedges for serving (optional)

Instructions:

Prepare Shrimp: Pat the shrimp dry with paper towels and season them with salt and pepper to taste.
Melt Butter: In a large skillet, melt the butter over medium heat.
Add Garlic: Once the butter is melted, add the minced garlic to the skillet. Cook for about 1 minute, stirring constantly, until the garlic is fragrant. Be careful not to let it burn.
Cook Shrimp: Add the olive oil to the skillet with the garlic butter. Increase the heat to medium-high. Add the seasoned shrimp to the skillet in a single layer. Cook for 2-3 minutes on each side, or until the shrimp are pink and opaque.
Season: Sprinkle chopped parsley over the shrimp and toss to coat evenly.
Serve: Transfer the garlic butter shrimp to a serving plate. Serve hot, garnished with additional parsley and lemon wedges if desired.
Enjoy: These garlic butter shrimp are delicious on their own or served over rice, pasta, or with crusty bread to soak up the flavorful butter sauce.

This recipe is quick to make and perfect for a weeknight dinner or a special occasion.

Enjoy your flavorful garlic butter shrimp!

Mushroom Risotto

Ingredients:

- 1 ½ cups Arborio rice
- 4 cups chicken or vegetable broth
- 1 cup dried porcini mushrooms
- 1 cup fresh mushrooms (such as cremini or button), sliced
- 1 small onion, finely chopped
- 2 cloves garlic, minced
- ½ cup dry white wine
- 1 cup grated Parmesan cheese
- 2 tablespoons butter
- 2 tablespoons olive oil
- Salt and pepper to taste
- Fresh parsley, chopped (for garnish)

Instructions:

Prepare Mushrooms: In a bowl, soak the dried porcini mushrooms in warm water for about 20-30 minutes until they are rehydrated. Once rehydrated, drain them, reserving the soaking liquid. Chop the rehydrated mushrooms.

Prepare Broth: In a saucepan, heat the chicken or vegetable broth over medium heat. Keep it warm while you prepare the risotto.

Sauté Mushrooms: In a large skillet or Dutch oven, heat the olive oil over medium heat. Add the fresh mushrooms and sauté until they are golden brown and tender, about 5-7 minutes. Remove the mushrooms from the skillet and set aside.

Sauté Aromatics: In the same skillet, add the chopped onion and minced garlic. Sauté until the onion is soft and translucent, about 3-4 minutes.

Toast Rice: Add the Arborio rice to the skillet with the onions and garlic. Stir to coat the rice with the oil and cook for 1-2 minutes until the rice is slightly toasted.

Deglaze with Wine: Pour in the dry white wine and stir, scraping up any browned bits from the bottom of the skillet. Cook until the wine has evaporated.

Add Mushrooms: Stir in the rehydrated porcini mushrooms and the sautéed fresh mushrooms.

Cook Risotto: Begin adding the warm broth to the skillet, one ladleful at a time, stirring frequently. Allow the rice to absorb the broth before adding more.

Continue this process until the rice is creamy and tender, but still slightly al dente, about 18-20 minutes.

Finish with Cheese and Butter: Once the risotto is cooked to your desired consistency, remove it from the heat. Stir in the grated Parmesan cheese and butter until melted and creamy. Season with salt and pepper to taste.

Serve: Garnish the mushroom risotto with chopped fresh parsley and additional grated Parmesan cheese, if desired. Serve hot and enjoy!

This mushroom risotto is rich, creamy, and packed with earthy mushroom flavor. It makes for a satisfying main course or a delicious side dish. Enjoy!

Blood Orange Margaritas

Ingredients:

- 2 ounces tequila
- 1 ounce triple sec or orange liqueur
- 2 ounces freshly squeezed blood orange juice
- 1 ounce freshly squeezed lime juice
- 1/2 ounce simple syrup (adjust to taste)
- Salt or sugar, for rimming the glass (optional)
- Ice
- Blood orange slices or lime wedges, for garnish

Instructions:

Rim the Glass (optional): If desired, rim the rim of your glass with salt or sugar. To do this, rub the rim of the glass with a lime wedge, then dip it into a plate of salt or sugar to coat the rim.

Mix Ingredients: In a cocktail shaker, combine the tequila, triple sec, blood orange juice, lime juice, and simple syrup. Add ice to the shaker.

Shake: Shake the ingredients vigorously for about 15-20 seconds until well-chilled.

Strain: Strain the margarita mixture into your prepared glass filled with ice.

Garnish: Garnish your blood orange margarita with a slice of blood orange or a lime wedge.

Serve: Serve immediately and enjoy your refreshing blood orange margarita!

Feel free to adjust the sweetness or tartness of the margarita by adding more or less simple syrup or adjusting the ratio of blood orange juice to lime juice. You can also experiment with different types of tequila to find your preferred flavor profile. Cheers!

Mini Quiche Lorraine

Ingredients:

- 1 package (about 9 ounces) of frozen mini tart shells (or you can make your own pastry)
- 6 slices of bacon, cooked and crumbled
- 1/2 cup shredded Swiss cheese
- 3 large eggs
- 1/2 cup heavy cream
- 1/4 cup whole milk
- 1/4 teaspoon salt
- 1/4 teaspoon black pepper
- Pinch of nutmeg
- 1 tablespoon chopped fresh chives (optional, for garnish)

Instructions:

Preheat Oven: Preheat your oven to 375°F (190°C).
Prepare Tart Shells: If using frozen mini tart shells, arrange them on a baking sheet. If making your own pastry, roll out the dough and cut into small circles to fit your mini tart pans. Press the dough into the pans, ensuring it covers the bottom and sides.
Add Fillings: Divide the crumbled bacon and shredded Swiss cheese evenly among the tart shells.
Prepare Egg Mixture: In a mixing bowl, whisk together the eggs, heavy cream, milk, salt, pepper, and nutmeg until well combined.
Fill Tart Shells: Carefully pour the egg mixture into each tart shell, filling them about 2/3 full.
Bake: Place the baking sheet with the filled tart shells in the preheated oven. Bake for about 20-25 minutes, or until the egg mixture is set and the crust is golden brown.
Cool and Garnish: Remove the mini quiches from the oven and let them cool slightly. If desired, garnish with chopped fresh chives for a pop of color and flavor.
Serve: Serve the Mini Quiche Lorraine warm or at room temperature. They are perfect for brunch, appetizers, or as a party snack.

These Mini Quiche Lorraine are versatile and can be customized with your favorite fillings. They're great for entertaining and can be made ahead of time, making them a convenient option for any gathering. Enjoy!

Spinach and Artichoke Dip

Ingredients:

- 1 (10-ounce) package frozen chopped spinach, thawed and drained
- 1 (14-ounce) can artichoke hearts, drained and chopped
- 1 cup shredded mozzarella cheese
- 1/2 cup grated Parmesan cheese
- 1/2 cup mayonnaise
- 1/2 cup sour cream or Greek yogurt
- 1 clove garlic, minced
- 1/2 teaspoon onion powder
- 1/4 teaspoon red pepper flakes (optional, for a bit of heat)
- Salt and pepper to taste
- Tortilla chips, crackers, or bread for serving

Instructions:

Preheat Oven: Preheat your oven to 375°F (190°C).
Prepare Spinach and Artichokes: Make sure the spinach is well drained. You can use paper towels to squeeze out excess moisture. Chop the artichoke hearts into bite-sized pieces.
Mix Ingredients: In a large mixing bowl, combine the chopped spinach, chopped artichoke hearts, shredded mozzarella cheese, grated Parmesan cheese, mayonnaise, sour cream or Greek yogurt, minced garlic, onion powder, and red pepper flakes (if using). Season with salt and pepper to taste.
Bake: Transfer the mixture to an oven-safe baking dish or skillet, spreading it out evenly. You can also sprinkle some extra mozzarella or Parmesan cheese on top if desired.
Bake in the preheated oven for about 25-30 minutes, or until the dip is hot and bubbly, and the cheese is melted and golden brown on top.
Serve: Remove the spinach and artichoke dip from the oven and let it cool for a few minutes before serving. Serve it warm with tortilla chips, crackers, or bread slices for dipping.
Enjoy: This creamy spinach and artichoke dip is sure to be a crowd-pleaser at your next gathering. It's perfect for game day, parties, or anytime you're craving a tasty appetizer.

Feel free to adjust the ingredients and seasonings according to your taste preferences. Enjoy!

Lobster Bisque

Ingredients:

- 2 lobsters (about 1 1/2 to 2 pounds each)
- 4 tablespoons unsalted butter
- 1 onion, chopped
- 2 carrots, chopped
- 2 celery stalks, chopped
- 2 cloves garlic, minced
- 2 tablespoons tomato paste
- 1/4 cup brandy or cognac
- 4 cups seafood or lobster stock
- 2 cups water
- 1 bay leaf
- 1/4 teaspoon paprika
- Pinch of cayenne pepper (optional, for heat)
- 1 cup heavy cream
- Salt and pepper to taste
- Chopped fresh chives or parsley for garnish

Instructions:

Prepare Lobsters: Bring a large pot of water to a boil. Add the lobsters and cook for about 8-10 minutes, or until they are bright red and cooked through. Remove the lobsters from the pot and let them cool slightly. Once cooled, remove the meat from the shells and chop it into bite-sized pieces. Reserve the shells for making stock.

Make Stock: In a large pot, melt 2 tablespoons of butter over medium heat. Add the lobster shells and cook, stirring occasionally, for about 5 minutes. Add the chopped onion, carrots, celery, and garlic to the pot. Cook for another 5 minutes, until the vegetables are softened.

Deglaze with Brandy: Stir in the tomato paste and cook for 1-2 minutes. Add the brandy or cognac to the pot, scraping up any browned bits from the bottom. Cook for a few minutes until the alcohol has evaporated.

Add Liquid: Pour in the seafood or lobster stock and water, then add the bay leaf, paprika, and cayenne pepper (if using). Bring the mixture to a simmer and let it cook for about 30-40 minutes, allowing the flavors to meld.

Blend and Strain: Once the stock has simmered, remove the pot from the heat and let it cool slightly. Use an immersion blender or transfer the mixture to a blender to puree until smooth. Strain the mixture through a fine-mesh sieve or cheesecloth, pressing down to extract as much liquid as possible. Discard the solids.

Finish the Bisque: Return the strained liquid to the pot and place it over medium heat. Stir in the chopped lobster meat and heavy cream. Cook for a few minutes until the soup is heated through. Season with salt and pepper to taste.

Serve: Ladle the lobster bisque into bowls and garnish with chopped fresh chives or parsley. Serve hot and enjoy!

This lobster bisque is rich, creamy, and full of flavor. It's perfect for a special dinner or any time you want to treat yourself to something delicious.

Mini Beef Wellingtons

Ingredients:

- 1 sheet puff pastry, thawed
- 4 beef tenderloin steaks, about 4-6 ounces each
- Salt and pepper to taste
- 2 tablespoons olive oil
- 2 tablespoons Dijon mustard
- 8 slices prosciutto or Parma ham
- 1 cup mushroom duxelles (finely chopped mushrooms sautéed with shallots and herbs until moisture evaporates)
- 1 egg, beaten (for egg wash)

Instructions:

Prepare the Beef:
- Season the beef tenderloin steaks generously with salt and pepper.
- Heat olive oil in a skillet over medium-high heat. Sear the steaks for about 1-2 minutes on each side, just until browned. Remove from heat and let them cool slightly.

Assembly:
- Roll out the puff pastry on a lightly floured surface. Cut it into squares, large enough to wrap around each steak.
- Spread a thin layer of Dijon mustard over each steak.
- Place a slice of prosciutto or Parma ham over the mustard.
- Spread a layer of mushroom duxelles over the ham.

Wrap the Steaks:
- Place each steak, mustard side down, in the center of each puff pastry square.
- Wrap the pastry around the steak, ensuring the edges are sealed tightly.
- Trim any excess pastry if necessary.

Chill:
- Place the wrapped steaks on a baking sheet lined with parchment paper.
- Brush the tops with beaten egg for a golden finish.
- Refrigerate the wrapped steaks for about 15-20 minutes to firm up.

Bake:
- Preheat the oven to 400°F (200°C).

- Once chilled, place the mini Beef Wellingtons in the preheated oven and bake for about 20-25 minutes, or until the pastry is golden brown and crispy.

Serve:
- Allow the mini Beef Wellingtons to cool slightly before serving.
- Serve them whole or sliced into smaller portions, depending on your preference.
- Enjoy!

These mini Beef Wellingtons are sure to impress your guests with their elegant presentation and delicious flavor. They're perfect for parties, gatherings, or even as a special treat for a cozy night in.

Blue Cheese and Walnut Crostini

Ingredients:

- Baguette, sliced into 1/2 inch thick rounds
- 1 cup crumbled blue cheese (such as Roquefort, Gorgonzola, or Stilton)
- 1/2 cup walnuts, chopped
- 2 tablespoons honey
- Fresh thyme leaves, for garnish (optional)
- Olive oil, for drizzling
- Salt and pepper to taste

Instructions:

Prepare the Baguette:
- Preheat your oven to 375°F (190°C).
- Arrange the baguette slices on a baking sheet in a single layer.
- Drizzle olive oil over each slice and season with a pinch of salt and pepper.

Toast the Baguette:
- Place the baking sheet in the preheated oven and bake for about 10-12 minutes, or until the baguette slices are golden brown and crisp.
- Remove from the oven and let them cool slightly.

Prepare the Blue Cheese and Walnut Topping:
- In a small bowl, mix together the crumbled blue cheese and chopped walnuts.
- Drizzle honey over the mixture and gently toss to combine. Adjust the amount of honey to taste, depending on how sweet you want the topping to be.

Assemble the Crostini:
- Once the baguette slices have cooled slightly, top each slice with a spoonful of the blue cheese and walnut mixture.
- If desired, garnish each crostini with fresh thyme leaves for an extra burst of flavor and visual appeal.

Serve:
- Arrange the prepared crostini on a platter and serve immediately.
- These crostini can be served warm or at room temperature, depending on your preference.

These Blue Cheese and Walnut Crostini are perfect for entertaining guests or enjoying as a tasty snack. The combination of creamy blue cheese, crunchy walnuts, and sweet honey atop crispy bread is simply irresistible!

Cucumber Avocado Rolls

Ingredients:

- 1 large cucumber
- 1 ripe avocado
- 1 tablespoon lemon juice
- Salt and pepper to taste
- Optional: thinly sliced smoked salmon, cooked shrimp, or crab meat
- Optional garnish: sesame seeds, chopped cilantro, or red pepper flakes

Instructions:

Prepare the Ingredients:
- Peel the cucumber and cut it lengthwise into thin slices using a vegetable peeler or a mandoline slicer. Aim for slices that are about 1/8 inch thick.
- Cut the avocado in half, remove the pit, and scoop out the flesh into a bowl. Mash the avocado with a fork and mix in the lemon juice, salt, and pepper. Adjust seasoning to taste.

Assemble the Rolls:
- Lay a cucumber slice flat on a clean surface.
- Spread a thin layer of mashed avocado onto the cucumber slice, leaving a small border around the edges.
- If desired, add a piece of smoked salmon, cooked shrimp, or crab meat on top of the avocado.

Roll the Cucumber Slices:
- Starting from one end, carefully roll up the cucumber slice, enclosing the avocado and any additional filling.
- Secure the roll with a toothpick if necessary to keep it from unraveling.
- Repeat the process with the remaining cucumber slices and avocado mixture.

Serve:
- Place the cucumber avocado rolls on a serving platter.
- Optional: Sprinkle sesame seeds, chopped cilantro, or red pepper flakes on top for added flavor and garnish.
- Serve immediately as a light appetizer or snack.

These cucumber avocado rolls are not only visually appealing but also incredibly tasty and nutritious. They're perfect for parties, picnics, or anytime you're craving a healthy and flavorful bite. Enjoy!

Apple Cider Glazed Pork Tenderloin

Ingredients:

- 1 pork tenderloin (about 1 to 1.5 pounds)
- Salt and pepper to taste
- 2 tablespoons olive oil
- 1 cup apple cider
- 2 tablespoons Dijon mustard
- 2 tablespoons honey
- 2 cloves garlic, minced
- 1 teaspoon dried thyme (or 1 tablespoon fresh thyme leaves)
- 1 tablespoon butter (optional)

Instructions:

Preheat the Oven:
- Preheat your oven to 375°F (190°C).

Prepare the Pork Tenderloin:
- Pat the pork tenderloin dry with paper towels. Season it generously with salt and pepper on all sides.

Sear the Pork Tenderloin:
- Heat olive oil in an oven-safe skillet over medium-high heat. Once the oil is hot, add the pork tenderloin and sear it for 2-3 minutes on each side until golden brown.

Make the Glaze:
- In a small bowl, whisk together the apple cider, Dijon mustard, honey, minced garlic, and dried thyme.

Glaze the Pork Tenderloin:
- Pour the apple cider glaze over the seared pork tenderloin, making sure to coat it evenly.

Roast in the Oven:
- Transfer the skillet to the preheated oven and roast the pork tenderloin for 15-20 minutes, or until it reaches an internal temperature of 145°F (63°C) for medium-rare or 160°F (71°C) for medium, as measured with a meat thermometer inserted into the thickest part of the meat.

Baste the Pork:
- Occasionally, baste the pork tenderloin with the glaze from the skillet to keep it moist and flavorful as it cooks.

Rest and Slice:

- Once cooked to your desired level of doneness, remove the pork tenderloin from the oven and let it rest for 5-10 minutes before slicing. This allows the juices to redistribute, resulting in a juicy and tender pork.

Optional: Make a Pan Sauce:
- If desired, you can make a simple pan sauce by adding a tablespoon of butter to the skillet with the remaining glaze. Cook it over medium heat, stirring constantly, until the sauce has thickened slightly.

Serve:
- Slice the pork tenderloin into medallions and drizzle with the pan sauce, if using. Serve hot and enjoy!

This apple cider glazed pork tenderloin is perfect for a special dinner or holiday meal.

The combination of flavors is sure to impress your family and friends!

Shrimp Scampi Linguine

Ingredients:

- 1 pound (450g) linguine pasta
- 1 1/2 pounds (680g) large shrimp, peeled and deveined
- Salt and pepper to taste
- 4 tablespoons unsalted butter
- 4 tablespoons olive oil
- 6 cloves garlic, minced
- 1/2 teaspoon red pepper flakes (adjust to taste)
- 1/4 cup white wine (optional)
- Zest and juice of 1 lemon
- 1/4 cup chopped fresh parsley
- Grated Parmesan cheese for serving

Instructions:

Cook the Linguine:
- Cook the linguine pasta according to the package instructions until al dente. Drain and set aside, reserving about 1/2 cup of pasta cooking water.

Prepare the Shrimp:
- Pat the shrimp dry with paper towels and season them with salt and pepper.

Cook the Shrimp:
- In a large skillet, heat 2 tablespoons of butter and 2 tablespoons of olive oil over medium-high heat.
- Add the shrimp to the skillet in a single layer and cook for about 2 minutes on each side, or until they are pink and opaque. Be careful not to overcook the shrimp. Once cooked, transfer them to a plate and set aside.

Make the Sauce:
- In the same skillet, add the remaining butter and olive oil.
- Add the minced garlic and red pepper flakes to the skillet and cook for about 1 minute, stirring constantly, until the garlic is fragrant. Be careful not to let the garlic brown.

Deglaze the Pan (Optional):
- If using white wine, pour it into the skillet and allow it to simmer for about 1 minute, scraping up any browned bits from the bottom of the pan.

Combine Shrimp and Sauce:

- Return the cooked shrimp to the skillet.
- Add the lemon zest and juice, chopped parsley, and cooked linguine to the skillet. Toss everything together until the shrimp and pasta are well coated in the sauce. If the sauce seems too thick, you can add some of the reserved pasta cooking water to loosen it up.

Serve:
- Divide the shrimp scampi linguine among serving plates.
- Garnish with additional chopped parsley and grated Parmesan cheese, if desired.
- Serve hot, and enjoy!

This Shrimp Scampi Linguine is a delicious and elegant dish that is perfect for a special dinner or any occasion. The combination of tender shrimp, garlic-infused sauce, and al dente linguine pasta is sure to delight your taste buds.

Caprese Salad Skewers

Ingredients:

- Cherry tomatoes
- Fresh mozzarella balls (bocconcini)
- Fresh basil leaves
- Balsamic glaze (store-bought or homemade)
- Extra virgin olive oil
- Salt and pepper to taste
- Wooden skewers

Instructions:

Prepare the Ingredients:
- Wash the cherry tomatoes and pat them dry with a paper towel.
- Drain the mozzarella balls if they are stored in liquid.
- Pick fresh basil leaves and rinse them under cold water. Pat them dry with a paper towel.

Assemble the Skewers:
- Take a wooden skewer and start by sliding on a cherry tomato.
- Follow the tomato with a mozzarella ball.
- Fold a basil leaf in half and add it to the skewer.
- Repeat the process until the skewer is filled, leaving a little space at each end for easy handling.

Arrange and Season:
- Place the assembled skewers on a serving platter.
- Drizzle the skewers with balsamic glaze and extra virgin olive oil.
- Sprinkle salt and pepper over the skewers to taste.

Serve:
- Serve the Caprese salad skewers immediately, or cover and refrigerate them until ready to serve.
- Optionally, you can serve them with additional balsamic glaze on the side for dipping.

These Caprese salad skewers are a perfect appetizer for parties, picnics, or any gathering. They are not only delicious but also visually appealing with vibrant colors and fresh flavors. Enjoy!

Raspberry Bellini

Ingredients:

- 1 cup fresh raspberries (plus extra for garnish)
- 1 tablespoon sugar (optional, adjust to taste)
- 1 bottle of Prosecco or other sparkling wine, chilled
- Fresh mint leaves for garnish (optional)

Instructions:

Prepare the Raspberry Purée:
- In a blender or food processor, combine the fresh raspberries and sugar (if using).
- Blend until smooth. If desired, you can strain the purée through a fine mesh sieve to remove the seeds for a smoother texture.

Assemble the Raspberry Bellini:
- Spoon 1-2 tablespoons of raspberry purée into the bottom of each champagne flute.
- Fill the glass about halfway with chilled Prosecco.
- Gently stir to combine the raspberry purée and Prosecco. Be careful not to overmix to avoid losing the bubbles.

Garnish and Serve:
- Garnish each glass with a fresh raspberry and a sprig of mint, if desired.
- Serve immediately while the Bellini is still bubbly and cold.

Variations:
- You can adjust the sweetness of the Bellini by adding more or less sugar to the raspberry purée, depending on your preference.
- For a non-alcoholic version, you can substitute sparkling water or lemon-lime soda for the Prosecco.

Presentation Tips:
- To make your Raspberry Bellinis even more visually appealing, you can rim the champagne flutes with sugar or decorate the glasses with additional raspberries on the rim.
- Serve the Bellinis in elegant champagne flutes to enhance the presentation.

Raspberry Bellinis are perfect for brunches, bridal showers, or any celebratory occasion. They are light, refreshing, and bursting with fruity flavor, making them a delightful addition to any gathering. Enjoy responsibly!

Gruyere and Thyme Stuffed Mushrooms

Ingredients:

- 12 large white button mushrooms, stems removed and reserved
- 1 tablespoon olive oil
- 2 cloves garlic, minced
- 1 small shallot, finely chopped
- Reserved mushroom stems, finely chopped
- 1/2 cup shredded Gruyere cheese
- 2 tablespoons fresh thyme leaves, chopped
- Salt and pepper to taste
- 2 tablespoons breadcrumbs (optional, for topping)
- Chopped fresh parsley for garnish (optional)

Instructions:

Prepare the Mushrooms:
- Preheat the oven to 375°F (190°C). Line a baking sheet with parchment paper.
- Remove the stems from the mushrooms and finely chop them. Set aside.

Prepare the Filling:
- Heat olive oil in a skillet over medium heat. Add the minced garlic and chopped shallot, and sauté for 2-3 minutes until softened.
- Add the chopped mushroom stems to the skillet and cook for an additional 3-4 minutes until they release their moisture and become tender. Remove from heat and let cool slightly.

Prepare the Filling:
- In a mixing bowl, combine the cooked mushroom mixture with shredded Gruyere cheese and chopped thyme leaves. Season with salt and pepper to taste.

Stuff the Mushrooms:
- Spoon the filling mixture generously into each mushroom cap, pressing down gently to compact the filling.

Bake the Stuffed Mushrooms:
- Place the stuffed mushrooms on the prepared baking sheet.
- Optional: Sprinkle breadcrumbs over the top of each stuffed mushroom for added texture.
- Bake in the preheated oven for 15-20 minutes, or until the mushrooms are tender and the filling is golden and bubbly.

Serve:
- Remove the stuffed mushrooms from the oven and let them cool slightly.
- Garnish with chopped fresh parsley, if desired, before serving.

These Gruyere and thyme stuffed mushrooms are perfect for parties, gatherings, or as an elegant appetizer for a special dinner. They are bursting with flavor and sure to impress your guests! Enjoy!

Antipasto Platter

Ingredients:

Meats:

- Prosciutto
- Salami (such as Genoa, Soppressata, or Pepperoni)
- Italian ham (such as Capicola or Mortadella)

Cheeses:

- Fresh mozzarella balls
- Sliced provolone
- Wedges of Parmesan or Pecorino Romano

Vegetables:

- Cherry tomatoes
- Marinated olives (such as Kalamata or Castelvetrano)
- Roasted red peppers
- Grilled artichoke hearts
- Marinated mushrooms
- Pickled vegetables (such as giardiniera)

Other Accompaniments:

- Breadsticks or grissini
- Slices of crusty Italian bread or baguette
- Crackers or breadsticks
- Extra virgin olive oil for dipping
- Balsamic glaze or reduction
- Fresh basil leaves for garnish

Instructions:

Prepare the Meats and Cheeses:
- Arrange the meats and cheeses on a large serving platter or wooden board, alternating between slices of meat and cheese for an appealing presentation.

Add the Vegetables:

- Fill in the gaps between the meats and cheeses with an assortment of vegetables, such as cherry tomatoes, olives, roasted red peppers, grilled artichoke hearts, marinated mushrooms, and pickled vegetables.

Add Other Accompaniments:
- Arrange breadsticks or grissini in a tall glass or alongside the platter.
- Place slices of crusty Italian bread or baguette in a basket or on a separate plate.
- Add crackers or breadsticks to complement the meats and cheeses.
- Place small bowls of extra virgin olive oil and balsamic glaze or reduction on the platter for dipping.

Garnish and Serve:
- Garnish the platter with fresh basil leaves for a pop of color and freshness.
- Serve the antipasto platter as a starter or appetizer before the main meal.

Serve and Enjoy:
- Invite your guests to help themselves to the array of flavors and textures on the platter.
- Pair the antipasto platter with a glass of wine, such as a light and fruity Pinot Grigio or a bold and robust Chianti.

This classic antipasto platter is perfect for entertaining guests or enjoying a relaxing evening with family and friends. It's versatile, customizable, and always a crowd-pleaser!

Pesto Pasta Salad

Ingredients:

- 12 ounces (about 340g) pasta of your choice (such as fusilli, penne, or farfalle)
- 1/2 cup basil pesto (store-bought or homemade)
- 1 cup cherry tomatoes, halved
- 1/2 cup cucumber, diced
- 1/4 cup red onion, finely chopped
- 1/4 cup black olives, sliced
- 1/4 cup roasted red peppers, diced
- 1/4 cup fresh mozzarella balls, halved (optional)
- Salt and pepper to taste
- Fresh basil leaves for garnish (optional)
- Grated Parmesan cheese for serving (optional)

Instructions:

Cook the Pasta:
- Bring a large pot of salted water to a boil. Cook the pasta according to the package instructions until al dente. Drain the pasta and rinse it under cold water to stop the cooking process. Drain well and transfer to a large mixing bowl.

Prepare the Vegetables:
- While the pasta is cooking, prepare the vegetables. Halve the cherry tomatoes, dice the cucumber, finely chop the red onion, slice the black olives, and dice the roasted red peppers. Set aside.

Assemble the Salad:
- Add the prepared vegetables to the bowl with the cooked pasta.
- Spoon the basil pesto over the pasta and vegetables.

Mix Well:
- Gently toss everything together until the pasta and vegetables are evenly coated with the pesto sauce.

Season to Taste:
- Taste the salad and season with salt and pepper as needed.

Chill (Optional):
- If time allows, cover the salad and refrigerate for at least 30 minutes to allow the flavors to meld together. This also allows the salad to cool if serving it cold.

Serve:

- Before serving, give the pasta salad a final toss.
- Optionally, garnish with fresh basil leaves and sprinkle with grated Parmesan cheese.
- Serve the pesto pasta salad as a side dish or as a light main course.

This pesto pasta salad is perfect for picnics, potlucks, or as a side dish for grilled meats or seafood. It's versatile, easy to make, and bursting with fresh flavors. Enjoy!

Fig and Goat Cheese Crostini

Ingredients:

- Baguette or French bread, sliced into 1/2-inch thick rounds
- Olive oil
- 8 ounces (225g) soft goat cheese
- 6-8 fresh figs, thinly sliced
- Honey, for drizzling
- Fresh thyme leaves, for garnish
- Balsamic glaze (optional, for drizzling)

Instructions:

Preheat the Oven:
- Preheat your oven to 375°F (190°C).

Toast the Bread:
- Place the baguette or French bread slices on a baking sheet in a single layer.
- Lightly brush each slice with olive oil on both sides.
- Bake in the preheated oven for 8-10 minutes, or until the bread is golden and crispy. Keep an eye on them to prevent burning.

Prepare the Goat Cheese:
- While the bread is toasting, spread a generous layer of goat cheese onto each toasted bread slice.

Add the Figs:
- Top each crostini with a few slices of fresh fig.

Drizzle with Honey:
- Drizzle honey over the figs on each crostini. The sweetness of the honey complements the flavors of the figs and goat cheese.

Optional: Balsamic Glaze:
- For an extra touch of flavor, you can drizzle a little balsamic glaze over the crostini. The sweet and tangy flavor pairs well with the other ingredients.

Garnish:
- Sprinkle fresh thyme leaves over the crostini for a pop of color and added flavor.

Serve:
- Arrange the fig and goat cheese crostini on a serving platter.
- Serve immediately as a delicious appetizer or starter.

These fig and goat cheese crostini are perfect for entertaining guests or enjoying as a special treat. They're elegant, flavorful, and easy to make, making them a great choice for any occasion. Enjoy!

Coconut Shrimp with Mango Dipping Sauce

Ingredients:

- 1 pound (about 450g) large shrimp, peeled and deveined
- 1 cup shredded coconut (sweetened or unsweetened)
- 1 cup panko breadcrumbs
- 2 eggs, beaten
- Salt and pepper to taste
- Vegetable oil, for frying

Instructions:

Prepare the Shrimp:
- Pat the shrimp dry with paper towels and season them with salt and pepper.

Coat the Shrimp:
- In separate bowls, place the beaten eggs, shredded coconut, and panko breadcrumbs.
- Dip each shrimp into the beaten eggs, then coat them in the shredded coconut and panko mixture, pressing gently to adhere.

Fry the Shrimp:
- In a large skillet, heat vegetable oil over medium-high heat until hot.
- Fry the coated shrimp in batches for 2-3 minutes on each side, or until they are golden brown and crispy.
- Transfer the fried shrimp to a plate lined with paper towels to drain any excess oil.

Mango Dipping Sauce:

Ingredients:

- 1 ripe mango, peeled and diced
- 2 tablespoons lime juice
- 2 tablespoons honey
- 1 tablespoon rice vinegar
- 1 teaspoon soy sauce
- 1/2 teaspoon grated fresh ginger
- Pinch of salt

Instructions:

Prepare the Mango Sauce:
- In a blender or food processor, combine the diced mango, lime juice, honey, rice vinegar, soy sauce, grated ginger, and a pinch of salt.
- Blend until smooth and well combined. If the sauce is too thick, you can add a little water to thin it out.

Adjust Seasoning:
- Taste the mango dipping sauce and adjust the seasoning if needed. Add more honey for sweetness or lime juice for acidity, according to your preference.

Serve:
- Transfer the mango dipping sauce to a serving bowl.
- Arrange the coconut shrimp on a platter and serve immediately with the mango dipping sauce on the side.

Presentation:

- Garnish the coconut shrimp with chopped fresh cilantro or sliced green onions for added flavor and presentation.
- Serve the coconut shrimp with mango dipping sauce as an appetizer or main dish, accompanied by steamed rice or a fresh salad.

Enjoy these crispy coconut shrimp with mango dipping sauce as a delicious and tropical-inspired dish!

Cranberry Brie Bites

Ingredients:

- 1 sheet puff pastry, thawed
- 4 ounces (about 113g) Brie cheese, rind removed, cut into small cubes
- 1/4 cup cranberry sauce (homemade or store-bought)
- 1 egg, beaten (for egg wash)
- Fresh thyme leaves, for garnish (optional)

Instructions:

Preheat the Oven:
- Preheat your oven to 375°F (190°C). Line a baking sheet with parchment paper.

Prepare the Puff Pastry:
- Roll out the thawed puff pastry sheet on a lightly floured surface.
- Using a sharp knife or pizza cutter, cut the puff pastry into squares, about 2 inches by 2 inches each.

Assemble the Brie Bites:
- Place a cube of Brie cheese in the center of each puff pastry square.
- Top the Brie with a small dollop of cranberry sauce.

Fold and Seal:
- Fold the corners of each puff pastry square over the Brie and cranberry filling, forming a small bundle.
- Press the edges together to seal the pastry.

Brush with Egg Wash:
- Place the assembled Brie bites on the prepared baking sheet.
- Brush the tops of the puff pastry with beaten egg using a pastry brush. This will give the pastry a golden color when baked.

Bake:
- Bake the Cranberry Brie Bites in the preheated oven for 15-18 minutes, or until the puff pastry is golden brown and crispy.

Garnish and Serve:
- Remove the Brie bites from the oven and let them cool slightly.
- Garnish with fresh thyme leaves, if desired.
- Serve the Cranberry Brie Bites warm as a delicious appetizer for your guests to enjoy.

These Cranberry Brie Bites are perfect for holiday gatherings, parties, or any special occasion. They are easy to make, elegant, and bursting with flavor. Enjoy!

Spicy Tuna Tartare

Ingredients:

- 8 ounces (225g) sushi-grade tuna, finely diced
- 1 ripe avocado, diced
- 1 tablespoon sesame oil
- 1 tablespoon soy sauce
- 1 teaspoon sriracha sauce (adjust to taste)
- 1 teaspoon lime juice
- 1 teaspoon toasted sesame seeds
- 1 green onion, thinly sliced (for garnish)
- Nori strips or wonton crisps (for serving, optional)

Instructions:

Prepare the Tuna:
- Ensure the tuna is fresh and sushi-grade. Use a sharp knife to finely dice the tuna into small cubes. Place the diced tuna in a mixing bowl.

Prepare the Seasonings:
- In a small bowl, whisk together the sesame oil, soy sauce, sriracha sauce, and lime juice until well combined.

Combine the Ingredients:
- Add the diced avocado to the bowl with the tuna.
- Pour the prepared seasoning mixture over the tuna and avocado.
- Gently toss everything together until the tuna and avocado are evenly coated with the seasoning mixture.

Chill (Optional):
- For best results, cover the tuna tartare mixture and refrigerate it for about 15-30 minutes to allow the flavors to meld together.

Serve:
- Once chilled, spoon the spicy tuna tartare onto serving plates or bowls.
- Sprinkle toasted sesame seeds over the top for added flavor and texture.
- Garnish with thinly sliced green onions.

Optional: Serve with Nori Strips or Wonton Crisps:
- To add crunch and texture to the dish, serve the spicy tuna tartare with nori strips or wonton crisps on the side.

Enjoy:
- Serve the spicy tuna tartare immediately as an appetizer or light meal.

- Enjoy the delicious combination of fresh tuna, creamy avocado, and spicy seasonings!

This spicy tuna tartare is perfect for sushi lovers or anyone who enjoys bold flavors. It's elegant, easy to prepare, and sure to impress your guests.

Glazed Meatballs

Ingredients:

For the Meatballs:

- 1 pound (about 450g) ground beef or a mixture of beef and pork
- 1/2 cup breadcrumbs
- 1/4 cup grated Parmesan cheese
- 1/4 cup milk
- 1 egg
- 2 cloves garlic, minced
- 1 teaspoon Italian seasoning
- Salt and pepper to taste
- Olive oil (for cooking)

For the Glaze:

- 1/2 cup ketchup
- 1/4 cup brown sugar
- 2 tablespoons apple cider vinegar
- 1 tablespoon Worcestershire sauce
- 1 teaspoon Dijon mustard
- Salt and pepper to taste

Optional Garnish:

- Chopped fresh parsley or green onions for garnish

Instructions:

Preheat the Oven:
- Preheat your oven to 375°F (190°C). Line a baking sheet with parchment paper or lightly grease it with oil.

Make the Meatballs:
- In a large mixing bowl, combine the ground meat, breadcrumbs, grated Parmesan cheese, milk, egg, minced garlic, Italian seasoning, salt, and pepper. Mix until well combined.
- Shape the mixture into meatballs, about 1 to 1.5 inches in diameter.

Cook the Meatballs:

- Heat a skillet over medium heat and add a little olive oil. Once the oil is hot, add the meatballs in batches, making sure not to overcrowd the pan. Cook the meatballs for 2-3 minutes on each side, or until browned and cooked through. Transfer the cooked meatballs to the prepared baking sheet.

Make the Glaze:
- In a small saucepan, combine the ketchup, brown sugar, apple cider vinegar, Worcestershire sauce, Dijon mustard, salt, and pepper. Stir well to combine.
- Cook the glaze over medium heat for 5-7 minutes, stirring occasionally, until it thickens slightly.

Glaze the Meatballs:
- Brush or spoon the glaze over the cooked meatballs, ensuring they are evenly coated.

Bake:
- Transfer the glazed meatballs to the preheated oven and bake for 10-12 minutes, or until the glaze is caramelized and bubbly.

Serve:
- Remove the glazed meatballs from the oven and let them cool slightly.
- Garnish with chopped fresh parsley or green onions, if desired.
- Serve the glazed meatballs hot as an appetizer or main dish, with toothpicks or alongside rice, pasta, or vegetables.

These glazed meatballs are perfect for parties, potlucks, or as a comforting family dinner. They're easy to make and packed with flavor! Enjoy!

Pear and Blue Cheese Salad

Ingredients:

- 2 ripe pears, cored and sliced thinly
- 4 cups mixed salad greens (such as baby spinach, arugula, or mixed lettuce)
- 1/2 cup crumbled blue cheese
- 1/4 cup chopped walnuts or pecans (optional)
- 2 tablespoons extra virgin olive oil
- 1 tablespoon balsamic vinegar
- Salt and freshly ground black pepper, to taste

Instructions:

In a large salad bowl, combine the mixed greens, sliced pears, crumbled blue cheese, and chopped nuts if using.
In a small bowl, whisk together the extra virgin olive oil and balsamic vinegar to make the dressing. Season with salt and pepper to taste.
Drizzle the dressing over the salad and toss gently to coat all the ingredients evenly.
Serve immediately as a side dish or light meal.

Optional variations:

- Add some thinly sliced red onions or shallots for extra flavor.
- Substitute other types of nuts like almonds or hazelnuts for the walnuts or pecans.
- Drizzle some honey over the salad for a touch of sweetness.
- Sprinkle some dried cranberries or pomegranate seeds for a burst of color and flavor.

Enjoy your delicious Pear and Blue Cheese Salad!

Mini Crab Cakes

Ingredients:

- 1 pound lump crabmeat, picked over for shells
- 1/2 cup breadcrumbs (panko breadcrumbs work well)
- 1/4 cup mayonnaise
- 1 large egg, beaten
- 2 tablespoons chopped fresh parsley
- 2 tablespoons Dijon mustard
- 1 tablespoon Worcestershire sauce
- 1 tablespoon lemon juice
- 1 teaspoon Old Bay seasoning
- Salt and pepper, to taste
- Olive oil, for frying

Instructions:

In a large bowl, gently combine the lump crabmeat, breadcrumbs, mayonnaise, beaten egg, chopped parsley, Dijon mustard, Worcestershire sauce, lemon juice, Old Bay seasoning, salt, and pepper. Be careful not to break up the crabmeat too much.

Form the mixture into small patties, about 1 1/2 inches in diameter, and place them on a baking sheet lined with parchment paper. You should get about 24 mini crab cakes from the mixture.

Heat a thin layer of olive oil in a large skillet over medium heat. Once the oil is hot, carefully place the mini crab cakes in the skillet, being careful not to overcrowd them. You may need to fry them in batches.

Cook the crab cakes for 2-3 minutes on each side, or until golden brown and crispy. Use a spatula to carefully flip them halfway through cooking.

Once cooked, transfer the mini crab cakes to a paper towel-lined plate to drain any excess oil.

Serve the mini crab cakes hot, garnished with lemon wedges and your choice of dipping sauce, such as tartar sauce, aioli, or cocktail sauce.

Enjoy your delicious Mini Crab Cakes as a tasty appetizer or snack!

Roasted Vegetable Platter

Ingredients:

Assorted vegetables, such as:

- Bell peppers (red, yellow, green)
- Zucchini
- Yellow squash
- Eggplant
- Cherry tomatoes
- Red onions
- Mushrooms
- Asparagus spears
- Carrots
- Broccoli florets
- Cauliflower florets
- Any other vegetables of your choice

For the marinade:

- 1/4 cup olive oil
- 2 cloves garlic, minced
- 1 tablespoon balsamic vinegar
- 1 teaspoon dried herbs (such as thyme, rosemary, or oregano)
- Salt and pepper, to taste

Optional toppings:

- Fresh herbs (such as parsley or basil), chopped
- Crumbled feta cheese
- Toasted pine nuts or chopped walnuts
- Balsamic glaze

Instructions:

Preheat your oven to 425°F (220°C). Line a large baking sheet with parchment paper or aluminum foil for easy cleanup.

Wash and prepare your assortment of vegetables. Cut them into bite-sized pieces, ensuring they are all roughly the same size for even cooking.

In a small bowl, whisk together the olive oil, minced garlic, balsamic vinegar, dried herbs, salt, and pepper to make the marinade.

Place the prepared vegetables in a large mixing bowl. Pour the marinade over the vegetables and toss until they are evenly coated.

Spread the vegetables out in a single layer on the prepared baking sheet.

Roast the vegetables in the preheated oven for 20-25 minutes, or until they are tender and slightly caramelized, stirring halfway through cooking.

Once roasted, transfer the vegetables to a serving platter. Sprinkle with optional toppings such as fresh herbs, crumbled feta cheese, toasted nuts, or a drizzle of balsamic glaze.

Serve the roasted vegetable platter warm or at room temperature as a delicious and colorful side dish or appetizer.

Enjoy your flavorful and nutritious Roasted Vegetable Platter!

Champagne Sorbet

Ingredients:

- 1 cup water
- 1 cup granulated sugar
- 2 cups Champagne or sparkling wine (choose a dry variety)
- 1/4 cup freshly squeezed lemon juice
- Zest of one lemon (optional, for extra flavor)
- Fresh berries or mint leaves, for garnish (optional)

Instructions:

In a small saucepan, combine water and granulated sugar. Heat over medium heat, stirring occasionally, until the sugar completely dissolves. This will make a simple syrup. Remove from heat and let it cool to room temperature.

Once the simple syrup has cooled, stir in the Champagne or sparkling wine, freshly squeezed lemon juice, and lemon zest (if using). Mix until well combined.

Pour the mixture into a shallow baking dish or a bowl with a wide surface area. Cover with plastic wrap and place it in the freezer.

After about an hour, check the sorbet mixture. It should start to freeze around the edges. Using a fork, gently scrape and stir the frozen edges into the liquid center. Repeat this process every 30 minutes to an hour for about 3-4 hours, or until the mixture is fully frozen and has a sorbet-like consistency. This step prevents the sorbet from becoming too icy and helps create a smooth texture.

Once the Champagne sorbet is frozen, it's ready to serve. Scoop it into serving bowls or glasses. Garnish with fresh berries or mint leaves if desired.

Serve immediately as a light and elegant dessert, or use it as a palate cleanser between courses during a multi-course meal.

Enjoy your homemade Champagne Sorbet!

Stuffed Jalapeños with Cream Cheese and Bacon

Ingredients:

- 12 jalapeño peppers
- 8 ounces cream cheese, softened
- 6 slices bacon, cooked and crumbled
- 1/2 cup shredded cheddar cheese
- 1/2 teaspoon garlic powder
- 1/2 teaspoon onion powder
- Salt and pepper, to taste
- Toothpicks, for securing the peppers (optional)

Instructions:

Preheat your oven to 375°F (190°C). Line a baking sheet with parchment paper or aluminum foil for easy cleanup.

Wash the jalapeño peppers and cut them in half lengthwise. Use a spoon to remove the seeds and membranes from each pepper, creating little jalapeño boats. Be sure to wear gloves while handling the peppers to avoid irritation from the capsaicin.

In a mixing bowl, combine the softened cream cheese, crumbled bacon, shredded cheddar cheese, garlic powder, onion powder, salt, and pepper. Mix until well combined.

Spoon the cream cheese mixture into each jalapeño half, filling them generously. If desired, you can wrap each stuffed jalapeño half with a half slice of bacon and secure it with a toothpick. This step is optional but adds extra flavor and texture.

Place the stuffed jalapeños on the prepared baking sheet, spacing them out evenly.

Bake in the preheated oven for 20-25 minutes, or until the jalapeños are tender and the filling is hot and bubbly.

Once cooked, remove the stuffed jalapeños from the oven and let them cool slightly before serving.

Serve the stuffed jalapeños warm as a delicious appetizer or party snack.

Enjoy your tasty Stuffed Jalapeños with Cream Cheese and Bacon!

Beef Sliders with Caramelized Onions

Ingredients:

For the sliders:

- 1 pound ground beef (preferably 80/20 lean to fat ratio)
- Salt and pepper, to taste
- Slider buns or mini burger buns
- Cheese slices (optional, such as cheddar or Swiss)

For the caramelized onions:

- 2 large onions, thinly sliced
- 2 tablespoons butter
- 1 tablespoon olive oil
- Salt and pepper, to taste
- 1 tablespoon brown sugar (optional, for extra sweetness)

Instructions:

Begin by caramelizing the onions. Heat the butter and olive oil in a large skillet over medium-low heat. Add the thinly sliced onions and cook them slowly, stirring occasionally, until they are soft and deeply golden brown, about 20-30 minutes. If desired, sprinkle the onions with a pinch of salt and pepper to enhance their flavor. Optionally, you can add brown sugar during the cooking process to further caramelize and sweeten the onions.

While the onions are caramelizing, prepare the beef sliders. Season the ground beef with salt and pepper in a mixing bowl. Divide the seasoned beef into small portions and shape them into mini burger patties, slightly larger than the slider buns as they will shrink slightly when cooked.

Heat a grill pan or skillet over medium-high heat. Cook the beef sliders for 2-3 minutes per side, or until they reach your desired level of doneness. If adding cheese, place a slice of cheese on each slider during the last minute of cooking, allowing it to melt slightly.

Assemble the sliders by placing a beef patty on the bottom half of each slider bun. Top with a spoonful of caramelized onions and the top half of the bun.

Serve the beef sliders immediately while warm. You can serve them as appetizers or as a main dish with your favorite side dishes.

Enjoy your delicious Beef Sliders with Caramelized Onions!

Pomegranate Mojitos

Ingredients:

- 1/2 cup fresh pomegranate seeds
- 8-10 fresh mint leaves, plus extra for garnish
- 2 tablespoons granulated sugar (adjust to taste)
- 1 lime, cut into wedges
- 2 ounces white rum
- 1/2 cup pomegranate juice
- Club soda or sparkling water
- Ice cubes
- Pomegranate arils and mint sprigs, for garnish (optional)

Instructions:

In a cocktail shaker or a tall glass, muddle together the fresh pomegranate seeds, mint leaves, granulated sugar, and lime wedges. Gently press down with a muddler or the back of a spoon to release the flavors and juices.
Add the white rum and pomegranate juice to the shaker or glass.
Fill the shaker or glass with ice cubes.
Shake the mixture vigorously if using a shaker, or stir well if using a glass, to combine all the ingredients and chill the mixture.
Strain the mixture into serving glasses filled with ice cubes. If you prefer a more rustic presentation, you can skip straining and leave the muddled ingredients in the glass.
Top each glass with club soda or sparkling water, filling to your desired level. Stir gently to combine.
Garnish each Pomegranate Mojito with a sprig of mint and a few fresh pomegranate arils for a pop of color and extra flavor.
Serve immediately and enjoy your refreshing Pomegranate Mojitos!

Feel free to adjust the sweetness and strength of the cocktail to suit your taste preferences. These cocktails are perfect for entertaining or enjoying a relaxing evening at home. Cheers!

Smoked Gouda and Apple Crostini

Ingredients:

- Baguette or French bread, sliced into 1/2-inch thick rounds
- Olive oil, for brushing
- 6 ounces smoked Gouda cheese, thinly sliced or shredded
- 1-2 apples (such as Granny Smith or Honeycrisp), thinly sliced
- Honey, for drizzling
- Fresh thyme leaves, for garnish (optional)

Instructions:

Preheat your oven to 375°F (190°C). Place the baguette or French bread slices on a baking sheet in a single layer.

Lightly brush both sides of the bread slices with olive oil.

Bake the bread slices in the preheated oven for 8-10 minutes, or until they are lightly golden and crispy. Remove from the oven and let them cool slightly.

While the bread slices are cooling, prepare the smoked Gouda cheese and apples. If using thinly sliced Gouda cheese, cut it into pieces that will fit nicely on top of the crostini.

Place a slice of smoked Gouda cheese on each bread slice.

Top each crostini with a slice of apple. You can arrange the apple slices neatly or overlap them slightly.

Drizzle a small amount of honey over each crostini to add sweetness and balance the flavors.

If desired, garnish the crostini with fresh thyme leaves for a pop of color and extra flavor.

Serve the Smoked Gouda and Apple Crostini immediately as a delicious appetizer or snack.

These crostini are perfect for parties, gatherings, or as a tasty treat for yourself. Enjoy the combination of savory cheese, sweet apples, and crunchy bread!

Teriyaki Chicken Wings

Ingredients:

For the Teriyaki Sauce:

- 1/2 cup soy sauce
- 1/4 cup water
- 1/4 cup brown sugar
- 2 tablespoons honey
- 2 cloves garlic, minced
- 1 teaspoon minced ginger
- 1 tablespoon cornstarch (optional, for thickening)

For the Chicken Wings:

- 2 pounds chicken wings, separated into drumettes and flats
- Salt and pepper, to taste
- Vegetable oil, for frying
- Sesame seeds and chopped green onions, for garnish (optional)

Instructions:

In a small saucepan, combine soy sauce, water, brown sugar, honey, minced garlic, and minced ginger to make the teriyaki sauce. Bring the mixture to a simmer over medium heat, stirring occasionally.

If desired, you can thicken the sauce by mixing cornstarch with a little water to make a slurry. Add the slurry to the simmering sauce and continue to cook, stirring constantly, until the sauce thickens slightly. Once thickened, remove the sauce from heat and set it aside.

Preheat your oven to 400°F (200°C). Line a baking sheet with parchment paper or aluminum foil for easy cleanup.

Season the chicken wings with salt and pepper to taste.

Heat vegetable oil in a large skillet or deep fryer over medium-high heat. Once the oil is hot, carefully add the chicken wings in batches, being careful not to overcrowd the skillet or fryer. Fry the wings for about 8-10 minutes, or until they are golden brown and crispy.

Remove the fried chicken wings from the oil and place them on a paper towel-lined plate to drain any excess oil.

Once all the wings are fried, transfer them to the prepared baking sheet. Brush the wings generously with the prepared teriyaki sauce, coating them evenly.

Bake the wings in the preheated oven for about 10-12 minutes, or until they are cooked through and the sauce is caramelized, brushing with additional sauce halfway through baking.

Once cooked, remove the wings from the oven and transfer them to a serving platter.

Garnish the teriyaki chicken wings with sesame seeds and chopped green onions, if desired.

Serve the wings hot as an appetizer or main dish, accompanied by extra teriyaki sauce for dipping.

Enjoy your delicious Teriyaki Chicken Wings!

Chocolate Truffles

Ingredients:

- 8 ounces (about 225 grams) good quality dark or milk chocolate, finely chopped
- 1/2 cup (120 ml) heavy cream
- 2 tablespoons (28 grams) unsalted butter, at room temperature
- Optional flavorings: vanilla extract, liqueur (such as rum, brandy, or Grand Marnier), espresso powder, etc.
- Coating options: cocoa powder, powdered sugar, chopped nuts, shredded coconut, melted chocolate for dipping, etc.

Instructions:

Place the chopped chocolate in a heatproof bowl.

In a small saucepan, heat the heavy cream over medium heat until it just begins to simmer. Be careful not to let it boil.

Pour the hot cream over the chopped chocolate and let it sit for about 1-2 minutes to soften the chocolate.

Gently stir the chocolate and cream together until the chocolate is completely melted and the mixture is smooth and glossy.

If desired, add any flavorings such as vanilla extract or liqueur to the chocolate mixture and stir until well combined.

Cut the butter into small pieces and gradually add them to the chocolate mixture, stirring until the butter is fully incorporated and the mixture is smooth.

Cover the bowl with plastic wrap and refrigerate the chocolate mixture for at least 2-3 hours, or until it is firm enough to handle and shape.

Once the chocolate mixture has chilled and firmed up, use a spoon or a small cookie scoop to portion out small amounts of the mixture. Roll each portion between your hands to form smooth balls, then place them on a baking sheet lined with parchment paper.

If desired, you can roll the truffles in various coatings such as cocoa powder, powdered sugar, chopped nuts, shredded coconut, etc. Alternatively, you can dip them in melted chocolate for a chocolate shell coating.

Once coated, place the truffles back on the parchment-lined baking sheet and refrigerate them for another 30 minutes to set.

Once set, transfer the chocolate truffles to an airtight container and store them in the refrigerator until ready to serve.

Enjoy your homemade chocolate truffles as a decadent treat or gift them to friends and loved ones!

These chocolate truffles can be customized with different flavorings and coatings to suit your taste preferences. Experiment with different combinations to create your perfect truffle!

Mini Fruit Tarts

Ingredients:

- 1 package of pre-made tart shells (you can also make your own if you prefer)
- Assorted fresh fruits (such as strawberries, blueberries, kiwi, raspberries, etc.)
- 1 package (8 oz) cream cheese, softened
- 1/4 cup powdered sugar
- 1 teaspoon vanilla extract
- Fruit glaze or apricot preserves (optional, for brushing over the fruit)

Instructions:

Prepare the Tart Shells:
- If using pre-made tart shells, follow the package instructions for baking, usually pre-bake them until they are golden brown. If making your own, follow your favorite tart shell recipe and bake accordingly. Allow them to cool completely before filling.

Prepare the Cream Cheese Filling:
- In a mixing bowl, beat the softened cream cheese until smooth.
- Add the powdered sugar and vanilla extract, then continue to beat until well combined and creamy. Set aside.

Prepare the Fruit:
- Wash and prepare your assortment of fresh fruits. Slice them thinly and set aside.

Assemble the Tarts:
- Once the tart shells have cooled, spoon the cream cheese mixture into each shell, filling them about halfway.

Arrange the Fruit:
- Carefully arrange the sliced fruits on top of the cream cheese filling in any pattern you like. Be creative!

Optional Glaze:
- If desired, you can brush a thin layer of fruit glaze or warmed apricot preserves over the top of the fruit to add shine and preserve freshness. This step is optional but adds a professional touch.

Chill and Serve:
- Once assembled, chill the mini fruit tarts in the refrigerator for at least 30 minutes to allow the cream cheese filling to set.
- Serve chilled and enjoy!

Feel free to customize this recipe by using your favorite fruits or adding additional flavors such as lemon zest or almond extract to the cream cheese filling. These mini fruit tarts are sure to impress at any gathering!